222
TIMELESS TRUTHS

AGELESS PRINCIPLES

BY KHARI SEKOU I

Dedicated To
The Memory Of

Thelma Wyatt Cummings Moore
aka SuperMom and Arthur B. Cummings, Sr. aka
Dadoo

Thank You

For Always Believing In Me

INTRODUCTION

This book is the sequel to 111 *Timeless Truths: Ageless Principles*. This is another collection of meditations, affirmations, quotes, ideas, and concepts to reflect on. They can be read and pondered one at a time, each day, or however you choose. It is my hope that the words in this book series can be a big source of inspiration and motivation to the readers.

Manifest Greatness,

Khari Sekou I

111timelesstruths.com

Truth 1

"One truth destroys a billion lies."

Truth 2

"This world has deceived us and we have deceived
ourselves. Stop believing the lies and
find the Truth."

Truth 3

"A lot of people don't want to show up for practice,
hard work, and training but will show up on the day
of the championship and expect a trophy."

Truth 4

"Those who truly want to win are willing
to do the work."

Truth 5

"Remember what's important."

Truth 6

"The false self is constantly pretending to be
the Real You. Knowing the difference
is critical."

Truth 7

"If you really want to change your situation
you will find a way to do it."

Truth 8

"To waste your time is to waste your life."

Truth 9

"We choose success or failure each day
with our actions."

Truth 10

"Unbelieve the lies."

Truth 11

"Persevere through the difficulty and the solution
will present itself."

Truth 12

"If you listen to your pain it will guide you
to your healing."

Truth 13

"You must accomplish your mission despite
the opposition."

Truth 14

—————•◦•—————

"Everyone is moving at their own pace and life
is not a race."

—————•◦•—————

Truth 15

"Hold people accountable but don't hold it against them."

Truth 16

"I assure you, no one will be talking about what kind of car you drive at your funeral."

Truth 17

"Getting angry won't change the situation."

Truth 18

"Put the work in and it will all work out."

Truth 19

"Truth will reveal itself to those who seek it."

Truth 20

"Turn off the television and turn on your consciousness."

Truth 21

"Protect your peace."

Truth 22

"People may be rude or they may be polite but always strive to do what is right."

Truth 23

"Deactivate the pain body."

Truth 24

"Close your eyes and listen to the silence."

Truth 25

"Change the way you see yourself."

Truth 26

"You will repeat the lesson until you complete
the lesson."

Truth 27

"When they left me for dead I began to truly live."

Truth 28

"The "easy way" is actually the hardest way."

Truth 29

"You call yourself rich but you never have time to do the things you love. Time is the real money."

Truth 30

"Use wealth wisely, not wastefully."

Truth 31

"The real will eventually be revealed."

Truth 32

"Remember to breathe."

Truth 33

"Playing it safe all the time is risky."

Truth 34

"Remember your dreams. Forget your nightmares."

Truth 35

"Don't rock the boat. Turn it over."

Truth 36

"The dark forces may hunt you and try to devour you throughout the night... but the Sun will certainly rise to eradicate the darkness."

Truth 37

"The wrong person in your bed will whisper the wrong things in your head."

Truth 38

"A Warrior finds peace on the battlefield."

Truth 39

"With tears in my eyes I will fight until I rise."

Truth 40

"When I was a child I was scared of the dark. Now
the dark is scared of me."

Truth 41

"Frustration and complaining are forms of powerlessness. Focus on solutions and take control of your situation."

Truth 42

"Change your thinking from what you have, to who
and what you are."

Truth 43

"When you hit rock bottom and you feel like you can't go on...you must go on."

Truth 44

"Listen to everyone that has something good to say."

Truth 45

"Seek Truth. Speak Truth."

Truth 46

"What you say with your mouth may be heard, but what you say with your actions speaks volumes."

Truth 47

"Love is invincible."

Truth 48

"You may not hold yourself accountable but I will."

Truth 49

"Come what may, find a way to enjoy your day."

Truth 50

"Breathe between each bite."

Truth 51

"They lied on me, to me, and through me for most of my life. They still lie on me and to me, but at least they can no longer lie through me."

Truth 52

"Live in the moment but never forget eternity."

Truth 53

"Quiet the storm that rages within you."

Truth 54

"Observe the chaos that surrounds you without being overwhelmed by it. Identify what needs to be done first and begin to restore order."

Truth 55

"Don't expect a harvest if you didn't plant the seeds."

Truth 56

"Outshine the master."

Truth 57

———————

"Justifying and rationalizing wrong won't
make it right."

———————

Truth 58

"If the truth will set you free, then the lie will definitely enslave you."

Truth 59

―――――――――

"Remember death."

―――――――――

Truth 60

"You may forget about death but death won't forget about you."

Truth 61

"The mind and the body were enjoying the
celebration, but the Soul left, and the party
was over immediately."

Truth 62

"The sincere and devoted student will eventually
become the Master."

Truth 63

"The True Master reveals the Mystery and gives us
the Victory."

Truth 64

―――――――――――――

"Civilize the savage within you."

―――――――――――――

Truth 65

"Bad habits come disguised as fun, but will still be with you when the fun is done."

Truth 66

"The only changes I plan to make are for the better."

Truth 67

"The problem is, we have learned the wrong way to live, and we are unwilling to change it."

Truth 68

———————

"You may think that you have more money than God,
but so did the last empire that was
reduced to ruins."

———————

Truth 69

"Your limiting beliefs will no longer limit you when
you stop believing in them."

Truth 70

"Don't rush the process. Trust the process."

Truth 71

"Fight for peace."

Truth 72

"I'd rather go the right way by myself, than go the wrong way with everyone else."

Truth 73

"If you don't want to see me win, you're not really my friend."

Truth 74

"Virtues will always have value."

Truth 75

"Clear out the weeds from the garden of your mind."

Truth 76

"Override your program and win."

Truth 77

"Be better than your best excuse."

Truth 78

"The hero that you hope will come to save you is within you. Reclaim your lost power."

Truth 79

"'When it all falls down, I will remain standing."

Truth 80

"Don't accept things the way they are
just because they are. If they can be better,
make them better."

Truth 81

"Meditation seems like punishment, but I should be able to close my eyes without constant chatter, negative emotions, anxiety, or the problems of the world interfering with my inner state."

Truth 82

"Conquer the weaknesses in your own self. Become undefeated."

Truth 83

"I stand like a mountain bold and unafraid."

Truth 84

"Discipline feels like prison, but it will lead you to freedom."

Truth 85

"You are your only competition. You win or lose against your "opponent" by being prepared, or unprepared for the battle."

Truth 86

"Learn from your past. Forgive yourself now. Move forward towards your future."

Truth 87

"How can we expect mercy when we are so bloodthirsty?"

Truth 88

"Destroy your weaknesses or they will destroy you."

Truth 89

"You go through what you're going through,
so you can become the person you are
meant to become."

Truth 90

"We are eternal beings trapped in time... the only freedom is to master the mind."

Truth 91

"When you change yourself, your world will change."

Truth 92

"The body is honest. The mind is lying.
The Soul is Truth."

Truth 93

"True Power is within you."

Truth 94

"On the chessboard of eternity, the greatest of kings are merely pawns."

Truth 95

———•———

"Most of us are looking for happiness from someone else. If they themselves don't have happiness, how can they give it to you?"

———•———

Truth 96

"Even if you live the life of your dreams, you will have to wake up one day."

Truth 97

"We as teachers are meant to pass the torch
to the next generation. Some teacher's
want to keep the torch to themselves.
The torch that they refuse to pass
will end up burning them."

Truth 98

"If you really want to win, you are willing to do the
work. If you're not willing to do the work,
can you really be mad if I move
forward without you?"

Truth 99

"While you were fast asleep, I painted my masterpiece."

Truth 100

"All we can do is to do all that we possibly can do."

Truth 101

"Some people want you to do for them what they won't even do for themselves."

Truth 102

"They say it's lonely at the top, but the spirit of victory is always with me."

Truth 103

"When I told them my plans they laughed. When they
saw me actually do it they cried.
I just smiled and kept going."

Truth 104

"If you want peace, be peaceful."

Truth 105

"The ones least qualified to lead are usually the ones that insist on being the leader. They will only lead themselves and others to their doom."

Truth 106

"Everyone is responsible but not everyone is
accountable."

Truth 107

―――――――•――――――•――――――

"The best revenge you can get is to make your life
beautiful again."

―――――――•――――――•――――――

Truth 108

"I'd rather know the painful ugly truth, than to believe the imaginary beautiful lie."

Truth 109

"You can buy everything in this matrix, but you can't buy Greatness."

Truth 110

"Man's quest for power will either bring out his best
or his worst qualities."

Truth 111

"Take your power back."

Truth 112

"Stop trying to be better than anyone else, and be better than you were yesterday."

Truth 113

———•———

"Your consciousness is supposed to lead your mind.
If your mind leads your consciousness, it will
only lead you to trouble."

———•———

Truth 114

"If it's not practiced regularly, it will deteriorate."

Truth 115

―――――••••――――

"You are much stronger than you think. You are far greater than you know."

―――――••••――――

Truth 116

"The day the enemy declared war on me, is the day
that I declared my victory."

Truth 117

"You can't be nice to everyone else and be mean to
yourself. Stop people pleasing.
You deserve better."

Truth 118

"You are a Lion. Stop pretending that you are not."

Truth 119

"I don't know how, and I don't know when, but I do know that I will win."

Truth 120

"It's easy to say, and simple to do, but it's hard to do it consistently until it becomes a habit."

Truth 121

"Who you are is more important than
what you have."

Truth 122

"Resisting life and trying to outsmart nature is futile.
The universe is undefeated."

Truth 123

"Filling yourself up with sensual enjoyments will only
leave you feeling empty."

Truth 124

"The body is already dead. The instant the Soul
leaves the body it will be burned or buried.
Know who and what you are."

Truth 125

"I once fell asleep inside my house. When I was awakened, my servant thought he was my master. I now have to remind him constantly that I'm in charge."

Truth 126

"The story we tell ourselves becomes our truth."

Truth 127

"What you think is the end of the world, may be the beginning of a new and better life."

Truth 128

"When you face your shadow, you will see the shadows of others at work. Conquering your own dark side will protect you from the dark side of other people."

Truth 129

"Something is wrong with the health system when you have more sick people than healthy people. The emergency rooms are full and so are the pharmaceutical companies' pockets."

Truth 130

"Western medicine has made an industry out of people's sickness. They have all the machines, high tech gadgets, and extravagant buildings, but the people are still sick and suffering. The buildings look better than the people."

Truth 131

"Modern man is more advanced than ancient man in technology and industry but more primitive in spirituality and morality."

Truth 132

"I wouldn't ask financial advice from someone who isn't wealthy...nor would I ask for health advice from a doctor who isn't healthy."

Truth 133

"It's best to have expectations clearly defined before starting any business or personal relationship. Lack of clarity leads to misunderstandings."

Truth 134

"You will never borrow your way out of debt."

Truth 135

"Business can ruin a friendship. Choose your
business partners wisely."

Truth 136

"Never do business with someone who's unwilling to write a business plan."

Truth 137

"If you were able to win without doing the work, it
would be unfair to all the people that
actually did it."

Truth 138

"Everybody's so busy. But what if we're all busy
doing the wrong things?"

Truth 139

"I saw a large crowd running so I started running
with them. Then I realized that they were all running
the wrong way."

Truth 140

"The ego never wants to admit when it's wrong, and acts like it knows what it doesn't know. If you allow this voice to guide you, it will destroy you."

Truth 141

"A good leader supports the endeavours of each member of their team, and leads by example."

Truth 142

"A teacher is great because of the impact they have
on their students, not because of the glory
they bring to themselves."

Truth 143

"Always accept the truth no matter who says it."

Truth 144

"You will find out who is really for you, if you judge
their character based on their actions,
not just their words."

Truth 145

"They tried to stop me at every step, but I just kept stepping."

Truth 146

"I will pick myself up once again.
I will continue."

Truth 147

"What if the whole world is wrong, and your heart is right?"

Truth 148

"Most people don't really want the truth...they just want you to agree with them."

Truth 149

"Do you just want to complain, or are you willing to change?"

Truth 150

"Find a way to forgive the people that wronged you, for your sake, so you can get on with your life."

Truth 151

"Open the blinds and let the light in. It's okay to live
your life again."

Truth 152

"There are some in your space that smile in your face, but they really want you to stay in your place."

Truth 153

"They wanted me to stay in my place, so I showed them where my place really was...the highest level of all."

Truth 154

"The people I thought were my friends gave up on me, but I didn't."

Truth 155

"This marathon started out with a lot of people. In the end it was just me and victory."

Truth 156

"The more you quit, the more you make it ok to quit.
Develop the habit of perseverance."

Truth 157

"I'd rather be alone with the Truth, than to be
surrounded by liars."

Truth 158

"May your light shine even brighter every time they try to dim it."

Truth 159

"Your mind is a supercomputer. Right now you're very likely running a program that you didn't choose and/or a toxic virus. Reformat the hard drive through meditation, and install a new operating system."

Truth 160

"A scarcity mindset will never produce
an abundant life."

Truth 161

"True love would never tear you down."

Truth 162

"They thought I was playing and I was...but I was playing on a much higher level."

Truth 163

"If you truly love someone, you want what's best for them...not just what's best for yourself."

Truth 164

"Destroy the house of lies that you currently occupy,
and build yourself a Mansion of Truth to live in."

Truth 165

———— • ————

"If you don't walk in your purpose, everyone around
you loses, including yourself."

———— • ————

Truth 166

"The more you succumb to negativity, the weaker you become."

Truth 167

"Hold yourself accountable."

Truth 168

"Sometimes things don't go right. But maybe one day they just might."

Truth 169

"Win or die."

Truth 170

"If you had to cheat, can you really say that you won?"

Truth 171

"Stop begging for likes on social media, and start liking yourself."

Truth 172

"Trusting a wolf, will eventually lead to being devoured."

Truth 173

"Nothing is as it seems, gotta see between. If even the dream is a scheme, how can freedom ring?"

Truth 174

"We've all been hurt and betrayed. I understand that you're still in pain, but the wounds will only fester if you don't allow them to heal."

Truth 175

—◦◦◦—

"They tried and tried to break my stride. They slandered my name with a billion lies. They plotted my demise to kill my pride. But the Lion inside will always rise."

—◦◦◦—

Truth 176

"What if the story you kept telling yourself
was a lie?"

Truth 177

"The people that you think are your friends, may be with you when you make bad decisions... but when the consequences come, you will be all alone."

Truth 178

"I internalized the world's negativity and became a prisoner of lies, pain, and fear. The more I meditate, the more I break the chains that once bound me."

Truth 179

"Refocus and Recenter."

Truth 180

"The enemies of humanity have studied you, but you haven't studied yourself. Thus, they are still able to manipulate you and control you psychologically."

Truth 181

"Bring your friends. Bring your enemies. We all end up in the same place eventually."

Truth 182

"I rose from that sunken place, sobered up from my drunken state, faced my shadows, and recovered my faith. I dared to change the hands of fate, and vowed to make my life something great."

Truth 183

"Everybody's waiting on a saviour, but we don't want
to change our behavior."

Truth 184

―――――――•••――――――――

"They once made a fool out of me. Now I make a wise man out of myself."

―――――――•••――――――――

Truth 185

"I have learned so much, yet I have so much to learn."

Truth 186

"The problem with living a lie is that the truth still exists, and it always will. Sooner or later, you will have to face it."

Truth 187

"When things get ugly, stay beautiful."

Truth 188

"Time keeps going no matter what. I suggest you do the same."

Truth 189

"Only go with the flow, when the flow is going in the
right direction."

Truth 190

"The more you sincerely seek to learn something, the more it will reveal its secrets to you."

Truth 191

"They used to talk about me like a dog. Now they talk about me like a Lion."

Truth 192

"We are all each other's teachers and students
in life."

Truth 193

"Set goal.
Move forward towards it.
Make mistakes.
Learn from them and make corrections.
Repeat until successful."

Truth 194

"You can party like there's no tomorrow, but
tomorrow will come. And when it does,
you will reap the fruits of the
seeds you planted today."

Truth 195

"Never lose sight of why you started doing what you are doing."

Truth 196

"I used to run from my fears, now I just run them
over and keep going."

Truth 197

―――・――

"A man is not weak but strong, that can admit when he's wrong."

―――・――

Truth 198

"My self worth isn't connected to my net worth."

Truth 199

"Those whose Souls are still sleeping, should not try to lead those who have been awakened."

Truth 200

"The heaven you seek is just on the other side
of this hell. Don't stop until you
get there."

Truth 201

"Get back to happy."

Truth 202

"We can create our inner heavens with our thoughts,
and the way that we respond to
what happens to us."

Truth 203

"You will know a righteous man by his actions, not just by his words."

Truth 204

———————•———————

"The problem isn't the problem. The problem is, you aren't focusing on the solutions."

———————•———————

Truth 205

"The stars in the night sky shine brilliantly beside
each other, without competing. Your
shine doesn't diminish mine."

Truth 206

"Who's right is not important.
What's right is."

Truth 207

"Momentum creates more momentum.
Get your project started, and that will create
more traction, and more opportunities."

Truth 208

"Somebody's perfect."

Truth 209

"Rethink the way you think about everything.
Rethink what you think is possible."

Truth 210

"I fed my fears to the lion that
was chasing me."

Truth 211

"Don't be afraid to start all the way over to do it a better way."

Truth 212

"Always be careful.
Never be fearful."

Truth 213

"Be conscious of your unconscious patterns and programming."

Truth 214

"When you don't know what you want out of life,
everything sounds like a good opportunity."

Truth 215

"The world is waiting for you to open the unique gift
that the Universe gave only to you."

Truth 216

"Life sometimes gives you what you don't want, so you can find out what it is that you do want."

Truth 217

"You may consider yourself superior or inferior to others, but death will treat us all equally."

Truth 218

"Modern society has mastered death and killing, but
has yet to master life and living."

Truth 219

"Travelers going to different destinations won't be together for long."

Truth 220

"When life gives you crap, use it as fertilizer in your
new garden...and make it beautiful."

Truth 221

"It may feel like life is dragging you and bringing out your worst. Come to realize that life is only pushing you to bring out your best."

Truth 222

"Your limiting beliefs only limit your own potential. If you only believed that you could do anything, then you could achieve the impossible."

About The Author:

Khari Sekou I is a visionary, gifted speaker, entrepreneur, martial artist, producer, and composer residing in Atlanta, GA. He focuses his energy on leadership roles and is an active member of his community. Due to his communication skills and positive messages, he is an in-demand public speaker.

To find out more, please visit Sekou's website:
www.111timelesstruths.com